I0442107

Magna Carta

Magna Carta

The Magna Carta was written by a group of 13th-century barons to protect their rights and property against a tyrannical king. It is concerned with many practical matters and specific grievances relevant to the feudal system under which they lived. The interests of the common man were hardly apparent in the minds of the men who brokered the agreement. But there are two principles expressed in Magna Carta that resonate to this day:

"No freeman shall be taken, imprisoned, disseised, outlawed, banished, or in any way destroyed, nor will We proceed against or prosecute him, except by the lawful judgment of his peers or by the law of the land."

"To no one will We sell, to no one will We deny or delay, right or justice."

Inspiration for Americans

During the American Revolution, Magna Carta served to inspire and justify action in liberty's defense. The colonists believed they were entitled to the same rights as Englishmen, rights guaranteed in Magna Carta. They embedded those rights into the laws of their states and later into the Constitution and Bill of Rights.

The Fifth Amendment to the Constitution ("no person shall . . . be deprived of life, liberty, or property, without due process of law.") is a direct descendent of Magna Carta's guarantee of proceedings according to the "law of the land."

John, by the Grace of God, King of England, Lord of Ireland, Duke of Normandy and Aquitaine, and Earl of Anjou, to his Archbishops, Bishops, Abbots, Earls, Barons, Justiciaries, Foresters, Sheriffs, Governors, Officers, and to all Bailiffs, and his faithful subjects, -- Greeting.

Know ye, that We, in the presence of God, and for t\he salvation of our own soul, and of the souls of all our ancestors, and of our heirs, to the honor of God, and the exaltation of the Holy Church and amendment of our Kingdom, by the counsel of our venerable fathers, Stephen Archbishop of Canterbury, Primate of all England, and Cardinal of the Holy Roman Church, Henry Archbishop of Dublin, William of London, Peter of Winchester, Joceline of Bath and Glastonbury, Hugh of Lincoln, Walter of Worcester, William of Coventry, and Benedict of Rochester, Bishops; Master Pandulph our Lord the Pope's Subdeacon and familiar, Brother Almeric, Master of the Knights-Templars in England, and of these noble persons, William Mareschal Earl of Pembroke, William Earl of Salisbury, William Earl of Warren, William Earl of Arundel, Alan de Galloway Constable of Scotland, Warin Fitz-Gerald, Hubert de Burgh Seneschal of Poictou, Peter Fitz-Herbert, Hugh de Nevil, Matthew Fitz-Herbert, Thomas Basset, Alan Basset, Philip de Albiniac, Robert de Roppel, John Mareschal, John Fitz-Hugh, and others our liegemen; have in the First place granted to God, and by this our present Charter, have confirmed, for us and our heirs forever:

That the English Church shall be free, and shall have her whole rights and her liberties inviolable; and we will this to be observed in such a manner, that it may appear from thence, that the freedom of elections, which was reputed most requisite to the English Church, which we granted, and by our Charter confirmed, and obtained the Confirmation of the same, from our Lord Pope Innocent the Third, before the rupture between us and our Barons, was of our own free will: which Charter we shall observe, and we will it to be observed with good faith, by our heirs forever.

We have also granted to all the Freemen of our Kingdom, for us and our heirs forever, all the underwritten Liberties, to be enjoyed and held by them and by their heirs, from us and from our heirs.

If any of our Earls or Barons, or others who hold of us in chief by military service, shall die, and at his death his heir shall be of full age, and shall owe a relief, he shall have his inheritance by the ancient relief; that is to say, the heir or heirs of an Earl, a whole Earl's Barony for one hundred pounds: the heir or heirs of a Baron for a whole Barony, by one hundred pounds; the heir or heirs of a Knight, for a whole Knight's Fee, by one hundred shillings at most: and he who owes less, shall give less, according to the ancient custom of fees.

But if the heir of any such be under age, and in wardship, when he comes to age he shall have his inheritance without relief and without fine.

The warden of the land of such heir who shall be under age, shall not take from the lands of the heir any but reasonable issues, and reasonable customs, and reasonable services, and the without destruction and waste of the men or goods, and if we commit the custody of any such lands to a Sheriff, or any other person who is bound to us for the issues of them and he shall make destruction or waste upon the ward-lands we will recover damages from him and the lands shall be committed to two lawful and discreet men of that fee, who shall answer for the issues to us, or to him to whom we have assigned them. And if we shall give or sell to anyone the custody of any such lands, and he shall make destruction or waste upon them, he shall lose the custody; and it shall be committed to two lawful and discreet men of that fee, who shall answer to us in like manner as it is said before.

But the warden, as long as he hath the custody of the lands, shall keep up and maintain the houses, parks, warrens, ponds, mills, and other things belonging to them, our of their issues; and shall restore to the heir when he comes of full age, his whole estate, provided with ploughs and other implements of husbandry, according as the time of Wainage shall require, and the issues of the lands can reasonably afford.

Heirs shall be married without disparagement, so that before the marriage be contracted, it shall be notified to the relations of the heir by consanguinity.

A widow, after the death of her husband, shall immediately, and without difficulty have her marriage and her inheritance; nor shall she give anything for her dower, or for her marriage, or for her inheritance, which her husband and she held at the day of his death: and she may remain in her husband's house forty days after his death, within which time her dower shall be assigned.

No widow shall be compelled to marry herself, while she is willing to live without a husband; but yet she shall give security that she will not marry herself without our consent, if she hold of us, or without the consent of the lord of whom she does hold, if she hold of another.

Neither we nor our Bailiffs, will seize any land or rent for any debt, while the chattels of the debtor are sufficient for the payment of the debt; nor shall the sureties of the debtor be compelled, while the principal debtor is able to pay the debt; and if the principal debtor fail in payment of the debt, not having wherewith to discharge it, the sureties shall answer for the debt; and if they be willing, they shall have the lands and rents of the debtor, until satisfaction be made to them for the debt which they had before paid for him, unless the principal debtor can shew himself acquitted thereof against the said sureties.

If anyone hath borrowed anything from the Jews, more or less, and die before that debt be paid, the debt shall pay no interest so long as the heir shall be under age, of whomsoever he may hold; and if that debt shall fall into our hands, we will not take anything except the chattel contained in the bond,

And if anyone shall die indebted to the Jews, his wife shall have her dower and shall pay nothing of that debt; and if children of the deceased shall remain who are under age, necessaries shall be provided for them, according to the tenement which belonged to the deceased and out of the residue the debt shall be paid, saving the rights of the lords. In like manner let it be with debts owing to others than Jews.

No scutage nor aid shall be imposed in our kingdom, unless by the common council of our kingdom; excepting to redeem our person, to make our eldest son a knight, and once to marry our eldest daughter, and not for these, unless a reasonable aid shall be demanded.

In like manner let it be concerning the aids of the City of London. -- And the City of London should have all its ancient liberties, and it's free customs, as well by land as by water. --Furthermore, we will and grant that all other Cities, and Burghs, and Towns, and Ports, should have all their liberties and free customs.

And also to have the common council of the kingdom, to assess and aid, otherwise than in the three cases aforesaid: and for the assessing of scutages, we will cause to be summoned the Archbishops, Bishops, Abbots, Earls, and great Barons, individually, by our letters. --And besides, we will cause to be summoned in general by our Sheriffs and Bailiffs, all those who hold of us in chief, at a certain day, that is to say at the distance of forty days, at the least, and to a certain place; and in all the letters of summons, we will express the cause of the summons: and the summons being thus made, the business shall proceed on the day appointed, according to the counsel of those who shall be present, although all who had been summoned have not come.

We will not give leave to anyone, for the future, to take an aid of his own free-men, except for redeeming his own body, and for making his eldest son a knight, and for marrying once his eldest daughter; and not that unless it be a reasonable aid.

No man shall be forced to perform more service for a knight's ee', or other free holding of land, than is due from it.

Ordinary lawsuits shall not follow the royal court around, but shall be held in a fixed place.

Trials upon the Writs of Novel Disseisin, Of Mort d'Ancestre, and Darrien Presentmen, shall not be taken but in their proper counties, and in this manner: --We, or our Chief Justiciary, if we are out of the kingdom, will send two Justiciaries into each county, four times in the year, who, with four knights of each county, chosen by the county, shall hold the aforesaid assizes, within the county on the day, and at the place appointed.

And if the aforesaid assizes cannot be taken on the day of the county-court, let as many knights and freeholders, of those who were present at the county-court remain behind, as shall be sufficient to do justice, according to the great or less importance of the business.

A freeman shall not be fined for a small offence, but only according to the degree of the offence; and for a great delinquency, according to the magnitude of the delinquency, saving his contenement: a Merchant shall be fined in the same manner, saving his merchandise, and a villain shall be fined after the same manner, saving to him his Wainage, if he shall fall into our mercy; and none of the aforesaid fines shall be assessed, but by the oath of honest men of the vicinage.

Earls and Barons shall not be fined but by their Peers, and that only according to the degree of their delinquency.

No Clerk shall be fined for his lay-tenement, but according to the manner of the others as aforesaid, and not according to the quantity of his ecclesiastical benefice.

All Counties, and Hundreds, Trethings, and Wapontakes, shall be at the ancient rent, without any increase, excepting in our Demesne-manors.

If anyone holding of us a lay-fee dies, and the Sheriff or our Bailiff, shall shew our letters-patent of summons concerning the debt which the defunct owed to us, it shall be lawful for the Sheriff or our Bailiff to attach and register the chattels of the defunct found on that lay-fee, to the amount of that debt, by the view of lawful men, so that nothing shall be removed from thence until our debt be paid to us; and the rest shall be left to the executors to fulfil the will of the defunct; and if nothing be owing to us by him, all the chattels shall fall to the defunct, saving to his wife and children their reasonable shares.

If any freeman shall die intestate, his chattels shall be distributed by the hands of his nearest relations and friends, by the view of the Church, saving to everyone the debts which the defunct owed.

No Constable nor other Bailiff of ours shall take the corn or other goods of anyone, without instantly paying money for them, unless he can obtain respite from the free will of the seller.

No Constable shall compel any Knight to give money for castle-guard, if he be willing to perform it in his own person, or by another able man, if he cannot perform it himself, for a reasonable cause: and if we have carried or sent him into the army, he shall be excused from castle-guard, according to the time that he shall be in the army by our command.

No Sheriff nor Bailiff of ours, nor any other person shall take the horses or carts of any freeman, for the purpose of carriage, without the consent of the said freeman.

Neither we, nor our Bailiffs, will take another man's wood, for our castles or other uses, unless by the consent of him to whom the wood belongs.

We will not retain the lands of those who have been convicted of felony, excepting for one year and one day, and then they shall be given up to the lord of the fee.

All kydells for the future shall be quite removed out of the Thames, and the Medway, and through all England, excepting upon the sea-coast.

The writ which is called Praecipe, for the future shall not be granted to anyone of any tenement, by which a freeman may lose his court.

There shall be one measure of wine throughout all our kingdom, and one measure of ale, and one measure of corn, namely the quarter of London; and one breadth of dyed cloth, and of russets, and of halberjects, namely, two ells within the lists. Also it shall be the same with weights as with measures.

Nothing shall be given or taken for the future for the Writ of Inquisition of life or limb; but it shall be given without charge, and not denied.

If any hold of us by Fee-Farm or Socage, or Burgage, and hold land of another by Military Service, we will not have the custody of the heir, nor of his lands, which are of the fee of another, on account of that Fee-Farm, or Socage, or Burgage; nor will we have the custody of the Fee-Farm, Socage or Burgage, unless the Fee-Farm owe Military Service. We will not have the custody of the heir, nor of the lands of anyone, which he holds of another by Military Service, on account of any Petty-Sergeantry which he holds of us by the service of giving us daggers, or arrows, or the like.

No Bailiff, for the future, shall put any man to his law, upon his own simple affirmation, without credible witnesses produced for the purpose.

No freeman shall be seized, or imprisoned, or dispossessed, or outlawed, or in any way destroyed; nor will we condemn him, nor will we commit him to prison, excepting by the legal judgement of his peers, or by the laws of the land.

All Merchants shall have safety and security in coming into England, and going out of England, and in staying and in travelling through England, as well by lands as by water, to buy and sell, without any unjust exactions, according to ancient and right customs, excepting the time of war, and if they be of a country at war against us: and if such are found in our land at the beginning of a war, they shall be apprehended without injury of their bodies and goods, until it be known to us, or to our Chief Justiciary, how the Merchants of our country are treated who are found in the country at war against us; and if ours be in safety there, the others shall be in safety in our land.

It shall be lawful to any person, for the future, to go out of our kingdom, and to return, safely and securely, by land or by water, saving his allegiance to us, unless it be in time of war, for some short space, for the common good of the kingdom: excepting prisoners and outlaws, according to the laws of the land, and of the people of the nation at war against us, and Merchants who shall be treated as it is said above.

If any hold of any escheat, as of the Honor of Wallingford, Nottingham, Boulogne, Lancaster, or of other escheats which are in our hand, and are Baronies, and shall die, his heir shall not give any other relief, nor do any other service to us, than he should have done to the Baron, if that Barony had been in the hands of the Baron; and we will hold it in the same manner that the Baron held it.

Men who dwell without the Forest, shall not come, for the future, before our Justiciaries of the Forest on a common summons; unless they be parties in a plea, or sureties for some person or persons who are attached for the Forest.

We will not make Justiciaries, Constables, Sheriffs, or Bailiffs, excepting of such as know the laws of the land, and are well disposed to observe them.

All Barons who have founded Abbies, which they hold by charters from the Kings of England, or by ancient tenure, shall have the custody of them when they become vacant, as they ought to have.

All evil customs of Forests and Warrens, and of Foresters and Warreners, Sheriffs and their officers, Water-banks and their keepers, shall immediately be inquired into by twelve Knights of the same county, upon oath, who shall be elected by good men of the same county; and within forty days after the inquisition is made, they shall be altogether destroyed by them never to be restored; provided that this be notified to us before it be done, or to our Justiciary, if we be not in England.

We will immediately restore all hostages and charters, which have been delivered to us by the English, in security of the peace and of their faithful service.

We will remove from their bailiwicks the relations of Gerard de Athyes, so that, for the future they shall have no bailiwick in England; Engelard de Cygony, Andrew, Peter, and Gyone de Chancell, Gyone de Cygony, Geoffrey de Martin, and his brothers, Philip Mark, and his brothers, and Geoffrey his nephew, and all their followers.

And immediately after the conclusion of the peace, we will remove out of the kingdom all foreign knights, cross-bow-men, and stipendiary soldiers, who have come with horses and arms to the molestation of the kingdom.

If any have been disseised or dispossessed by us, without a legal verdict of their peers, of their lands, castles, liberties, or rights, we will immediately restore these things to them; and if any dispute shall arise on this head, then it shall be determined by the verdict of the twenty-five Barons, of whom mention is made below, for the security of the peace. --Concerning all those things of which anyone hath been disseised or dispossessed, without the legal verdict of his peers by King Henry our father, or King Richard our brother, which we have in our hand, or others hold with our warrants, we shall have respite, until the common term of the Crusaders, excepting those concerning which a plea had been moved, or an inquisition taken, by our precept, before our taking the Cross; but as soon as we shall return from our expedition, or if, by chance, we should not go upon our expedition, we will immediately do complete justice therein.

The same respite will we have, and the same justice shall be done, concerning the disafforestation of the forests, or the forests which remain to be disafforested, which Henry our father, or Richard our brother, have afforested; and the same concerning the wardship of lands which are in another's fee, but the wardship of which we have hitherto had, occasioned by any of our fees held by military service; and for Abbies founded in any other fee than our own, in which the Lord of the fee hath claimed a right; and when we shall have returned, or if we shall stay from our expedition, we shall immediately do complete justice in all these pleas.

No man shall be apprehended or imprisoned on the appeal of a woman, for the death of any other man than her husband.

All fines that have been made by us unjustly, or contrary to the laws of the land; and all fines that have been imposed unjustly, or contrary to the laws of the land, shall be wholly remitted, or ordered by the verdict of the twenty-five Barons, of whom mention is made below, for the security of the peace, or by the verdict of the greater part of them, together with the aforesaid Stephen, Archbishop of Canterbury, if he can be present, and others whom he may think fit to bring with him: and if he cannot be present, the business shall proceed, notwithstanding, without him; but so, that if anyone or more of the aforesaid twenty-five Barons have a similar plea, let them be removed from that particular trial, and others elected and sworn by the residue of the same twenty-five, be substituted in their room, only for that trial.

If we have disseised or dispossessed any Welshmen of their lands, or liberties, or other things, without a legal verdict of their peers, in England or in Wales, they shall be immediately restored to them; and if any dispute shall arise upon this head then let it be determined in the Marches by the verdict of their peers: for a tenement of England, according to the law of England; for a tenement of Wales, according to the law of Wales; for tenement of the Marches, according to the law of the Marches. The Welsh shall do the same to us and to our subjects.

Also concerning those things of which any Welshman hath been disseised or dispossessed without the legal verdict of his peers, by King Henry our father, or King Richard our brother, which we have in our hand, or others hold with our warrant, we shall have respite, until the common term of the Crusaders, excepting for those concerning which a plea had been moved, or an inquisition made, by our precept, before our taking the cross. But as soon as we shall return from our expedition, or if, by chance, we should not go upon our expedition, we shall immediately do complete justice therein, according to the laws of Wales, and the parts aforesaid.

We will immediately deliver up the son of Llewelin, and all the hostages of Wales, and release them from their engagements which were made with us, for the security of the peace.

We shall do to Alexander King of Scotland, concerning the restoration of his sisters and hostages, and his liberties and rights, according to the form in which we act to our other Barons of England, unless it ought to be otherwise by the charters which we have from his father William, the late King of Scotland; and this shall be by the verdict of his peers in our court.

But since we have granted all these things aforesaid, for GOD, and for the amendment of our kingdom, and for the better extinguishing the discord which has arisen between us and our Barons, we being desirous that these things should possess entire and unshaken stability forever, give and grant to them the security underwritten; namely, that the Barons may elect twenty-five Barons of the kingdom, whom they please, who shall with their whole power, observe, keep, and cause to be observed, the peace and liberties which we have granted to them, and have confirmed by this our present charter, in this manner: that is to say, if we, or our Justiciary, or our bailiffs, or any of our officers, shall have injured anyone in anything, or shall have violated any article of the peace or security, and the injury shall have been shown to four of the aforesaid twenty-five Barons, the said four Barons shall come to us, or to our Justiciary if we be out of the kingdom, and making known to us the excess committed, petition that we cause that excess to be redressed without delay. And if we shall not have redressed the excess, or, if we have been out of the kingdom, our Justiciary shall not have redressed it within the term of forty days, computing from the time when it shall have been made known to us, or to our Justiciary if we have been out of the kingdom, the aforesaid four Barons, shall lay that cause before the residue of the twenty-five Barons; and they, the twenty-five Barons, with the community of the whole land, shall distress and harass us by all the ways in which they are able; that is to say, by the taking of our castles, lands, and possessions, and by any other means in their power, until the excess shall have been redressed, according to their verdict; saving harmless our person, and the persons of our Queen and children; and when it hath been redressed, they shall behave to us as they have done before.

And whoever of our land pleaseth, may swear, that he will obey the commands of the aforesaid twenty-five Barons, in accomplishing all the things aforesaid, and that with them he will harass us to the utmost of his power: and we publicly and freely give leave to everyone to swear who is willing to swear; and we will never forbid any to swear. But all those of our land, who, of themselves, and of their own accord, are unwilling to swear to the twenty-five Barons, to distress and harass us together with them, we will compel them by our command, to swear as aforesaid.

And if anyone of the twenty-five Barons shall die, or remove out of the land, or in any other way shall be prevented from executing the things above said, they who remain of the twenty-five Barons shall elect another in his place, according to their own pleasure, who shall be sworn in the same manner as the rest.

In all those things which are appointed to be done by these twenty-five Barons, if it happen that all the twenty-five have been present, and have differed in their opinions about anything, or if some of them who had been summoned, would not, or could not be present, that which the greater part of those who were present shall have provided and decreed, shall be held as firm and as valid, as if all the twenty-five had agreed in it: and the aforesaid twenty-five shall swear, that they will faithfully observe, and, with all their power, cause to be observed, all the things mentioned above.

And we will obtain nothing from anyone, by ourselves, nor by another, by which any of these concessions and liberties may be revoked or diminished. And if any such thing shall have been obtained, let it be void and null: and we will never use it, neither by ourselves nor by another.

And we have fully remitted and pardoned to all men, all the ill-will, rancor, and resentments, which have arisen between us and our subjects, both clergy and laity, from the commencement of the discord. Moreover, we have fully remitted to all the clergy and laity, and as far as belongs to us, have fully pardoned all transgressions committed by occasion of the said discord, from Easter, in the sixteenth year of our reign, until the conclusion of the peace.

And, moreover, we have caused to be made to them testimonial letters-patent of the Lord Stephen, Archbishop of Canterbury, the Lord Henry, Archbishop of Dublin, and of the aforesaid Bishops, and of Master Pandulph concerning this security, and the aforesaid concessions.

Wherefore, our will is and we firmly command that the Church of England be free, and that the men in our kingdom have and hold the aforesaid liberties, rights, and concessions, well and in peace, freely and quietly, fully and entirely, to them and their heirs, of us and our heirs, in all things and places, forever as is aforesaid.

It is also sworn, both on our part, and on that of the Barons, that all the aforesaid shall be observed in good faith, and without any evil intention. Witnessed by the above, and many others.

Given by our hand in the Meadow which is called Runningmead, between Windsor and Staines, this 15th day of June, in the 17th year of our reign.

Page Left blank

www.ingramcontent.com/pod-product-compliance
Lightning Source LLC
Chambersburg PA
CBHW081548280526
45788CB00010B/3403